MOTORMANIA

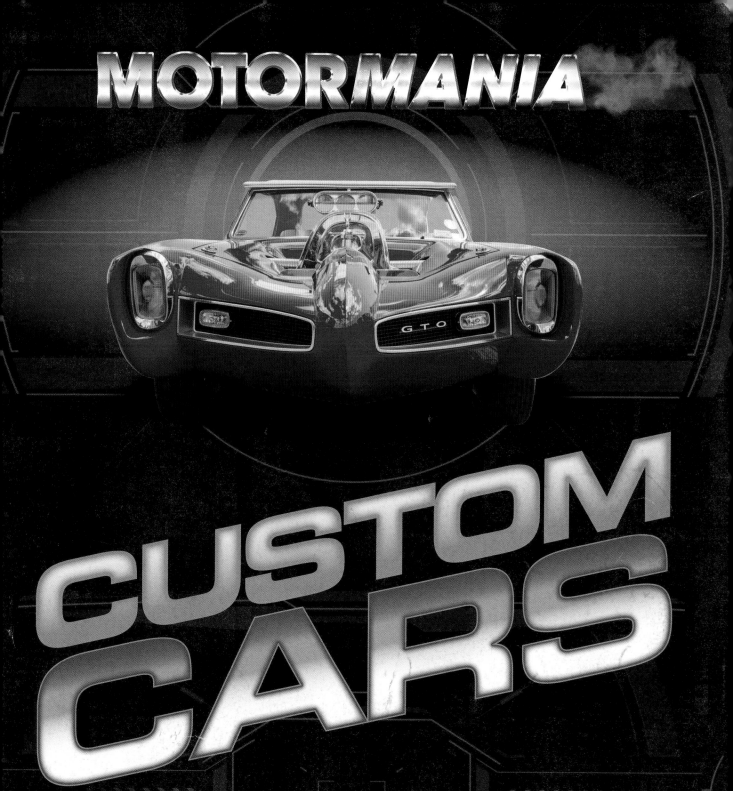

CUSTOM CARS

ROB COLSON

WAYLAND
www.waylandbooks.co.uk

First published in Great Britain
in 2020 by Wayland

Series editor: John Hort
Produced by Tall Tree Ltd
Designer: Jonathan Vipond

HB ISBN: 978 1 5263 1316 4
PB ISBN: 978 1 5263 1317 1

Wayland
An imprint of Hachette Children's Group
Part of Hodder and Stoughton
Carmelite House
50 Victoria Embankment
London EC4Y 0DZ

An Hachette UK Company
www.hachette.co.uk
www.hachettechildrens.co.uk

Printed and bound in China

Picture Credits

t-top, b-bottom, l-left, r-right, c-centre, fc-front cover,
bc-back cover
fc 13b Sipa/Shutterstock, bc Historic Vehicle Association, 2t, 11b
Steve Bruckmann / Shutterstock.com, 2c, 20
Tokumeigakarinoaoshima/CC, 1, 2b, 14-15t, 14-15b, 18b Erin
Cadigan / Shutterstock.com, 3b, 17t Combatbot2015/CC, 4b
Galyna Andrushko / Shutterstock.com, 4-5 Lamborghini, 5
WENN Rights Ltd / Alamy Stock Photo, 6b Kevin M. McCarthy /
Shutterstock.com, 6-7 Bloomberg / Getty Images, 7 Keith Bell /
Shutterstock.com, 8-9 Historic Vehicle Association, 8b, 9t Rik
Hoving, Custom Car Chronicle, 9b Maksim Toome /
Shutterstock.com, 10l Ford Motor Company, 10b Scalhotrod,
10-11 Jennifer Graylock / Ford Motor Company, 12t, 12b Roberto
Galan / Shutterstock.com, 13t Toshifumi Hotchi / Shutterstock.
com, 13b Sipa/Shutterstock, 14cl Eric Rickman/The Enthusiast
Network via Getty Images/Getty Images, 15r Freesek/CC, 16-17
Royalbroil/CC, 17b Michael Heilman / Shutterstock.com, 18-19t
Dan Jamieson / Shutterstock.com, 19t XRISTOFOROV /
Shutterstock.com, 19b Oto Godfrey and Justin Morton/CC, 21t
DY5W-sport/CC, 21b Ilya Plekhanov/CC, 22bl Joost J. Bakker
from Ijmuiden/CC, 22-23 Reinhardt and Co / Shutterstock.com,
23t Pan_photo / Shutterstock.com, 23b Ogletree / Shutterstock.
com, 24-25 Kenji Thuloweit / U.S. Air Force, 25cr U.S. Air Force,
25b Master Sgt. Scott Reed / U.S. Air Force, 26-27, 32 Sergey Kohl
/ Shutterstock.com, 27b Devkotlan Photography / CC, 28-29t,
28-29b BMW, 29b Kgbo / CC
Every attempt has been made to clear copyright. Should
there be any inadvertent omission, please apply to the
publisher for rectification.

CONTENTS

WHAT IS A CUSTOM CAR?

Custom cars are ordinary cars that have been modified into one-of-a-kind vehicles. They may be changed to add speed, style or all-weather performance. Some custom cars have become famous for their unique designs.

Hot rod enthusiasts gather to race each year on the Bonneville Salt Flats in Utah, USA.

HOT RODS

Hot rods are American custom cars that have been modified for speed. The engines of the original cars are often replaced with more powerful ones, while body parts, such as the bonnet, bumpers or mudguards, are removed or cut down to save weight. First made in the 1930s by criminals smuggling alcohol keen to outrun the police, hot rods have been used for racing since the 1950s.

SPECIAL EDITIONS

Some new cars come with a wide range of options so that their owners can customise them to their precise needs. Lamborghini built just five models of their exclusive US$4.5 million **supercar**, the Veneno. Each one was made to its owner's specifications, with custom interior, body kit and paint job.

The Veneno Roadster is an open-top version of the supercar.

MOVIE CARS

Some of the wildest and wackiest custom cars have been made especially for TV or movies. In the 1960s and 1970s, many custom cars were built for TV shows. One of the most memorable was the Panthermobile, created for *The Pink Panther Show* (1960–1978). Measuring 7 metres long, it was built around the **chassis** of an Oldsmobile Tornado.

The driver of the Panthermobile sat in front of the front wheels.

FORD MODEL T
T-BUCKET

The Model T was the world's first mass-produced car. More than 15 million Model Ts were made between 1908 and 1927. As an affordable car with widely available parts, it became a popular choice among hot rod builders, creating custom cars known as 'T-Buckets'.

KOOKIE'S KAR

The T-Bucket was invented in the 1950s by Hollywood actor and hot rod enthusiast Norm Grabowski. He took the body of a Model T and gave it a powerful Cadillac engine. Grabowski's car became famous when it appeared in the TV show *77 Sunset Strip*. It was known as Kookie's Kar, after a character in the show.

TECH POINT

T-Buckets look very different from the original Model T (right). Grabowski created his hot rod from two Ford cars, a 1922 Model T and a 1931 Model A. He shortened the body of the Model T and added parts from the Model A to the back. He cut down the chassis of the Model T to create a nose-down, tail-up look.

Huge 5.4-litre engine has twin **superchargers**.

T-BUCKET

YEAR CREATED:
Kookie's Kar made in 1955

ORIGINAL MODEL:
Ford Model T

Six gleaming chrome exhaust pipes were added along the side.

MODERN T-BUCKETS
Today, the original Model T bodies have mostly worn out and are extremely rare. For this reason, modern T-Buckets are normally built using replica **fibreglass** bodies. A large engine is added at the front, and a Model T-style radiator is fitted in front of it. The windscreen is typically a vertical glass pane, as in the original car.

HIROHATA MERC

In the early 1950s, the Mercury Eight was a popular model with custom car builders. The Hirohata Merc is a custom 1951 Mercury Eight **coupé**. It is named after its original owner Bob Hirohata, who drove the car to shows across the United States.

THE HIROHATA MERC

YEAR CREATED:

1953

ORIGINAL MODEL:

Mercury Eight coupé

Narrow side windows are the result of the lowered roof.

The custom paint job required 30 layers of paint.

Valves are above
the cylinders.

The grille teeth
in the side trim were
taken from a 1952 Chevrolet.

TECH POINT

TECH POINT

Hirohata replaced the original Mercury side-valve engine with a more advanced Cadillac overhead-valve engine, calling his resulting car a 'Mercillac'. In the Cadillac engine, the **valves** controlling the flow of fuel were placed directly above the **cylinders** rather than to the side. This kind of engine was expensive to make, but was efficient and powerful.

SLEEK LOOK

The car was customised for Hirohata by Los Angeles-based brothers Sam and George Barris. George would later create the Batmobile (see pages 10–11). They created a sleek outline by lowering the roof and curving the rear window forwards. They added **side skirts** taken from a Buick, which were painted a darker colour to emphasise the new lines.

REPLICAS

Today, custom car builders continue to be inspired by the Barris brothers' design, creating fibreglass replicas of the Hirohata Merc's body.

LINCOLN FUTURA

BATMOBILE

This one-off custom car was made for Batman to drive in the 1960s TV series. The Batmobile was created by George Barris, co-creator of the Hirohata Merc (pages 8–9), by modifying a 1950s concept car.

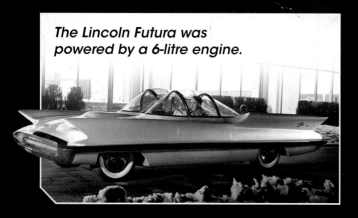

The Lincoln Futura was powered by a 6-litre engine.

CONCEPT CAR

The Batmobile was made by customising a Lincoln Futura. This was a concept car that had been exhibited at auto shows in 1955, showing off push-button controls and a futuristic double-dome canopy. After appearing in the 1959 movie *It Started with a Kiss*, the Futura had been bought by George Barris and was sitting in his Hollywood shop.

GEORGE BARRIS

George Barris (1925–2015) was given just three weeks to make the Batmobile. With such little time, he chose to modify his Futura rather than building a car from scratch. He submitted drawings of his design, including the distinctive batwing tail fins and grille designed to look like a bat's face, to the US Patent Office so that nobody else would be able to copy it.

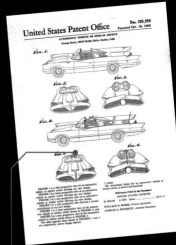

The drawings detail the car's unique design.

The Batmobile kept the Futura's double-dome.

Red lines emphasise the car's sleek shape.

BATMOBILE

YEARS CREATED:
1966

ORIGINAL MODEL:
Lincoln Futura

Tail fins were shaped like bat wings.

BATMAN'S GADGETS
The Batmobile was kitted out with a range of gadgets for Batman to use, such as the Batphone, most of which was just for show. However, some features that really worked were added, including a **propane** furnace that made the Batmobile's tail spit out flames and smoke.

CHEVROLET
LOWRIDER

A lowrider is a custom car that can dance. Fitted with extreme **suspension** systems, it can bounce up and down or side to side. Lowriders can be made out of many different models, but the Chevrolet Impala is a favourite.

LOWRIDER

YEARS CREATED:
From 1959

ORIGINAL MODEL:
Various, but especially the Chevrolet Impala

SPECIAL SUSPENSION

The first lowriders were made by Mexican Americans in Los Angeles, California in the 1950s. The cars were made as low as possible by cutting down the suspension and weighing them down. In 1959, extremely low cars were made illegal, so the customisers came up with a clever solution. They gave their lowriders **hydraulic** suspensions so that they could rise up or lower down on command.

Lowrider suspension operates using a hydraulic actuator. This is a chamber that can be quickly filled with liquid. A compressor shoots liquid into the actuator, making it expand rapidly. This creates a sudden force that pushes one side of the car high into the air. The actuators use a lot of energy, and are powered by extra car batteries.

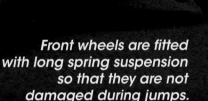

Front wheels are fitted with long spring suspension so that they are not damaged during jumps.

HOP COMPETITIONS

Lowrider owners show off their cars' moves at hop competitions that attract thousands of spectators. Moving their cars by remote control, they can make the nose of the car leap more than 2 metres into the air, jiggle the car from side to side or bounce the rear. The cars are marked for their tricks and their custom paint jobs.

PONTIAC GTO
MONKEEMOBILE

This elongated custom car was created for the pop band The Monkees to drive in their 1960s hit TV show. Two versions were made: one for filming and another to be driven around the United States on promotional tours. Both Monkeemobiles were made from converted Pontiac GTOs.

ROOM FOR THE BAND

Inside the car, designer Dean Jeffries (1933–2013, left) created extra room by removing the boot and fuel tank, adding a third row of seats and extending the roof. He tilted the windscreen upwards and added chrome trimming.

The nose was stretched by more than 30 cm.

SHARK-LIKE

Dean Jeffries lengthened both ends of the car with sheet metal. He attached two grilles, separated by a curved nose, to give the front of the car a shark-like appearance. A chrome-plated supercharger reared out of the centre of the bonnet to complete the look.

An original 1966 Pontiac GTO

TECH POINT

Jeffries removed the suspension from the rear **axle** and placed weights at the rear. This meant that most of the weight was at the back, allowing the car to do stunt wheelies. However, it made the car very difficult to handle, and none of the band members were able to drive it safely!

The canvas roof resembled that of a Ford Model T.

MONKEEMOBILE

YEAR CREATED:

1966

ORIGINAL MODEL:

Pontiac GTO **convertible**

FORD F-250
BIGFOOT

Bigfoot is a customised pick-up truck that marked the invention of a whole new kind of vehicle: the monster truck. With huge wheels and extreme suspension, monster trucks wow crowds with their amazing stunts, including car crushes and tricks, such as wheelies.

Bigfoot 15 jumps over a row of crushed cars at a Monster XL show in 2015.

FIRST BIGFOOT

The original Bigfoot was created in 1979 by Bob Chandler, a car dealer from St Louis in the US. He made it by modifying a 1974 Ford F-250 pickup truck, replacing its undercarriage with one taken from a large military loader. Chandler showed off his new creation at local car shows.

CAR CRUSH

In 1981, Chandler videoed himself performing a car crush, driving over a line of old cars in Bigfoot. The video proved so popular that he started to perform the stunt in front of crowds. Seeing this, other truck owners started creating their own monster trucks, and soon the monster truck show was born.

BIGFOOT

YEAR CREATED:
1979

ORIGINAL MODEL:
Ford F-250 pickup

BIGGEST EVER

Since creating the original model, Chandler's company have made more than 20 Bigfoot monster trucks. The biggest of all is Bigfoot 5. Fitted with 3-m-wide tyres and standing nearly 5 metres high, Bigfoot 5 is officially the tallest, widest and heaviest pickup truck in the world.

TECH POINT

A heavy-duty suspension is key to the abilities of monster trucks. The huge wheels are attached to the strong tubular chassis using a combination of springs and **shock absorbers** that give up to 1.2 metres of suspension travel. This long-travel suspension is crucial to cushion the landing after a stunt, such as a wheelie.

Hydraulic shock absorber

DMC DELOREAN

TIME MACHINE

The Time Machine was a customised DMC DeLorean sports car created for the *Back to the Future* movies (1985–1990). In total, five different DeLoreans were used in the three movies. Since then, custom car enthusiasts have made dozens of replica Time Machines.

For one scene, liquid nitrogen was poured over the car to make it look really cold.

ROUGH AND READY

The Time Machine was created by adding extra parts to represent its fictional abilities. Aircraft parts such as blinking lights were added, while the base of its nuclear reactor was made from the hubcap of a Dodge Polara. The car was intended to look messy. The designers wanted it to appear as if the Time Machine had been constructed in a garage by its fictional creator, Doc Brown.

TECH POINT

Back to the Future director Robert Zemeckis chose the DeLorean because he thought its 'gull-wing' doors made it look like a spaceship. The doors are hinged at the top, and look like the wings of a gull when they are open. The weight of the doors is supported by torsion bars. These are metal bars that twist when the doors are closed and untwist as the doors open to help lift them up.

Flashing lights were added at the back.

FICTIONAL POWER UNIT

Inside, the Time Machine was fitted with a control panel to operate its fictional features. These included the 'flux capacitor' that allowed the car to travel in time, with a digital panel that showed the change in the year. In the first movie, the Time Machine was powered by a nuclear reactor, but in later films it was fitted with a Mr. Fusion generator, which created power from household waste.

TIME MACHINE

YEAR CREATED:

1985

ORIGINAL MODEL:

DMC DeLorean

The boxes at the rear were part of the flux capacitor. They were made from jet exhausts.

KEI TRUCK
SUZUKI CARRY

Front bumper is fitted with a 'bucktooth lip' spoiler.

Kei cars and trucks are small Japanese vehicles with tiny engines. The Suzuki Carry is a kei truck that can be put to a wide variety of uses. Some are customised for a practical purpose, while others have been modified simply to stand out from the crowd.

SMALL AND CHEAP

In Japan, kei cars and trucks have special yellow licence plates. These show that the vehicles comply with the kei rules, which impose strict limits on size and weight. In a country where parking space is limited and road taxes are expensive, kei cars and trucks are given special discounts due to their size.

KEI TRUCK

YEARS CREATED:

2013–present

ORIGINAL MODEL:

Suzuki Carry

TECH POINT

Kei trucks are not allowed engines larger than 660 cc – about the size of the engine on a large motorbike. They have a maximum length of 3.4 metres and width of 1.48 metres. To make the most of their power and size, the body panels are made of ultra-thin metal, while the small engine sits underneath the driver.

HELLO SPECIAL

Custom car specialists Hello Special have created a Suzuki Carry with scissor doors that slide upwards like the doors of a Lamborghini (see page 25). To complete the look, it has wide bumpers, curvy mudguards and a shiny golden paint job.

VARIED USES

In many Asian countries, Suzuki Carrys have been customised to become taxis, with room in the back for four passengers. In Japan, Carrys may be specially adapted for fishing trips or to act as mobile market stalls. Some have even been modified into miniature fire engines.

CHRYSLER JEEP
CUSTOM JEEPS

The Jeep Wrangler is a compact sports utility vehicle (SUV) built for off-road driving. Some owners fit their Jeeps with new custom components that can deal with extreme conditions.

A large 'bull bar' at the front of this Jeep protects it from collisions.

CUSTOM JEEP

YEARS CREATED:

1943 (Jeeps from any era can be customised)

ORIGINAL MODEL:

Jeep Wrangler

WILLY'S JEEP

The original Willy's Jeep was made in 1943. Developed for the US Army during the Second World War (1939–1945), it was a cheap but tough off-road vehicle, ideal for heavy duty jobs such as carrying weapons or acting as a field ambulance. After the war, the Jeep was sold to the public, and it became the first mass-produced four-wheel-drive car.

TECH POINT

To cope with uneven surfaces, custom Jeeps can be fitted with lift kits. A custom suspension lifts the chassis by up to 10 cm to give extra **clearance**. Each wheel is fitted with its own flexible arm, allowing the wheels to point at different angles as the car negotiates a large obstacle. The car becomes a little harder to control, but it can tackle rougher terrain.

FLEXIBLE VEHICLE

The Jeep Wrangler is a flexible off-road vehicle. The roof can be removed, and it can even be driven with the doors off and the windscreen folded forwards. Custom parts make it even more flexible, providing extra protection or extra toughness.

Special tyres give extra grip on snow and ice.

Winch to pull the car if it gets stuck.

Larger wheels give extra strength to take on steep hills.

FORD MUSTANG
AIRFORCE X-1

EXTRA POWER
*The engine generates 500 **horsepower**. It is made more powerful by mixing nitrous oxide rather than air with the fuel to burn it.*

In 2009, the US Air Force teamed up with custom car specialists Galpin Auto Sports to produce a car for their shows. The result was the X-1 Supercar, a heavily modified Ford Mustang. From the outside it looks like a sports car, but the interior has been transformed into a cockpit like that of a fighter jet.

CARBON-FIBRE PARTS
*On the outside, the car has been given **carbon-fibre** trim. The body has been widened to fit the extra-wide wheels, also made from carbon fibre.*

TECH POINT

The X-1 is fitted with scissor doors, which open vertically at a fixed hinge at the front of the doors. Scissor doors are also known as 'Lambo doors' after the Lamborghini Countach, the first production car to feature them. On wide cars, scissor doors save space, allowing the passenger and the driver to climb in and out in narrow parking spots.

COCKPIT

The driver is strapped in at the centre of the car on a fully operational ejector seat. The car is controlled using a joystick taken from an aircraft, giving an even greater sense that you are inside a fighter jet. The dashboard is touchscreen-operated and features a display for night vision.

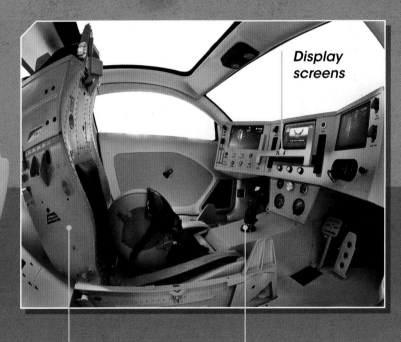

Display screens

Ejector seat

Joystick control

AIRFORCE X-1 MUSTANG

YEAR CREATED:
2009

ORIGINAL MODEL:
Ford Mustang

BAJA BUG

Baja Bugs are customised Volkswagen Beetles, which are known as 'Bugs' in the USA. Named after a desert area in southern California, Baja Bugs are specially modified to be driven off-road in the open desert.

At the back, the engine is completely exposed to allow it to stay as cool as possible.

THE FIRST BAJA BUG

In 1968, Gary Emory, an employee at a Volkswagen dealership in southern California, wanted to build a car he could race in the desert. He created the first Baja Bug by stripping down an old Beetle and rebuilding it from scratch, using new parts he sourced from work. Emory added a tubular steel cage, rugged suspension, and larger off-road wheels and tyres.

TECH POINT

In 1969, as the Baja Bug grew popular, fibreglass body part kits, known as 'bug eye' kits were produced. These allowed custom builders to fit a ready-made lightweight new body to their cars. Today, dealers provide a wide range of parts specially made for Baja Bugs, including off-road suspension, steering and brake systems, and wheels and tyres.

The body is lifted from the ground to provide clearance on rough desert terrain.

BAJA BUG

YEAR CREATED:
1968

ORIGINAL MODEL:
Volkswagen Beetle

BAJA 1000
The Baja Bug made its racing debut in 1968 at the Baja 1000 in Mexico, one of the most famous off-road races in the world. The race is held on a course through the Baja California Desert, with different classes for cars, trucks, motorbikes and buggies. Today, many Baja Bugs compete in the buggy class each year.

BMW i3

CUSTOM ELECTRIC CARS

The i3 is German manufacturer BMW's all-electric five-door hatchback. The company offers a range of special options for the car, adapting it for use as an emergency response vehicle. The cars are customised with equipment to suit the needs of a particular urban area.

BMW i3

YEARS CREATED:
2013–present

ORIGINAL MODEL:
BMW i3

The small electric cars form part of a rapid emergency response unit.

to an emergency.

POLICE CAR

Police officers in Wädenswil, Switzerland, patrol the streets in specially equipped BMW i3 The cars are fitted with front and rear flash lights and a ro LED display that can give signals such as 'Accident' or 'Please follow'. The cars also have a hands-free microphor system to allow the driver to make public announcement

FIRE CAR

In 2016, BMW provided a fleet of 52 customised i3s to the London Fire Brigade. Fitted with blue emergency lights, these new fire cars form part of a city-wide campaign in London to reduce exhaust emissions by going electric. The next stage will be to replace fire engines with all-electric models.

CAR SHARE

In Warsaw, Poland, the authorities are battling smog with an innovative car-share scheme, operated entirely by smart phone. Customers can pick up one of 500 specially equipped BMW i3s from parking spots across the city and drop them off anywhere they like.

GLOSSARY

Axle
A central rod to which the wheels of a car are attached. A four-wheeled car has two axles – one at the front and another at the rear.

Carbon fibre
A strong but lightweight material made from ultra-thin strands of carbon that have been woven together.

Chassis
The strong frame of a car to which the engine, wheels and body are attached.

Clearance
The distance between the ground and the bottom of the body of a car.

Convertible
Also known as a roadster, a car with a detachable roof.

Coupé
A car with a fixed roof and two doors.

Cylinders
The parts of an engine inside which fuel burns to pump pistons and generate power.

Fibreglass
A strong, lightweight material made of a mixture of plastic and glass fibres.

Horsepower
A unit of measurement for power, or the rate at which work is done. One horsepower is roughly equal to the power of one strong horse.

Hydraulics
A power system in which fluids are used to transfer force from one place to another.

Propane
A highly flammable gas that is used as a bottled fuel. Propane is made during the processing of natural gas and petroleum.

Shock absorber
A part of a vehicle's suspension that absorbs the energy of bumps and vibrations.

Side skirts
Panels on the sides of a car that are intended to help produce downforce to keep the car safely on the road.

Supercar
A high-performance sports car that is made in small numbers and sells for a very high price. Supercars are the fastest road-legal cars in the world.

Supercharger
A device attached to an engine that increases the pressure of the air that is fed into the cylinders. This helps the fuel to burn, increasing the power of the engine.

Suspension
A system of springs and shock absorbers that attach the wheels to a car's chassis.

Valve
A device that allows liquid or air to flow in one direction but not in the other. Valves are fitted to a car's engine to control the intake of fuel and air and the output of exhaust fumes.

FACT FILE

FAMOUS CUSTOM CARS AND THEIR MAKERS

CUSTOM CAR	ORIGINAL MODEL	YEAR MADE	BUILT BY	BUILT FOR	DISTINCTIVE FEATURE
Hirohata Merc	Mercury Eight	1953	Sam and George Barris	Owner Bob Hirohata	Sleek bodywork
Kookie's Kar (T-Bucket)	Ford Model T	1955	Norm Grabowski	77 Sunset Strip TV Show	Powerful engine low to the ground
Batmobile	Lincoln Futura	1966	George Barris	Batman TV show	Gadgets, including a propane burner and a parachute
Monkeemobile	Pontiac GTO	1966	Dean Jeffries	The Monkees TV show	Ability to perform wheelies
Baja Bug (original)	Volkswagen Beetle	1968	Gary Emory	Racing in the desert	Rugged suspension
Panthermobile	Oldsmobile Tornado	1969	Joe Bailon, Bill Hines and Bill Honda	The Pink Panther Show	Open driving compartment
Bigfoot Monster Truck (original)	Ford F-250	1979	Bob Chandler	Truck shows	Huge wheels and long suspension
Time Machine	DMC DeLorean	1985	Ron Cobb and Andrew Probert	Back to the Future movie trilogy	Time travel machinery
Airforce X-1	Ford Mustang	2009	Galpin Auto Sports	US Air Force shows	Fully functioning ejector seat
Hello Special	Suzuki Carry	2016	Hello Special	Display at car shows	Scissor doors

INDEX